Transformative Love

A Healing Guide for Intimate Relationships

Hugo W. Elfinstone

PublishAmerica
Baltimore

© 2005 by Hugo W. Elfinstone.

All rights reserved. No part of this book may be reproduced, stored in a retrieval system or transmitted in any form or by any means without the prior written permission of the publishers, except by a reviewer who may quote brief passages in a review to be printed in a newspaper, magazine or journal.

First printing

ISBN: 1-4137-8747-9
PUBLISHED BY PUBLISHAMERICA, LLLP
www.publishamerica.com
Baltimore

Printed in the United States of America

I dedicate this book to Mom for teaching me how to love!

And to Baby Jessica who reminds me of what love is!

And to Snookie for being my best friend and loving partner!

Acknowledgments

I would like to thank Amy Potter for her love and help with organizing and editing of this book. I would like to thank Amy Silver for organizing and editing *Love That Lasts*, which grew into this book (*Transformative Love*). Also for what I learned about love and relationship from her. I would like to thank Betsy Dew for her support and suggesting that I submit this book to PublishAmerica. I would like to thank Sandy Wood for teaching me self-love and how to heal a broken heart. I would like to thank Jane Mullen who has taught me about Love, Oneness and what is really important in life! I would like to thank Brad Blanton (*Radical Honesty*) for training me in honesty, gestalt therapy, and how to clean up the past. I would like to thank James Yates for teaching me about creative group work. I would like to thank Jerry Griffin for showing me an example of being a loving, honest, and compassionate human being. I would like to thank Scott Throckmorton for being a role model of how to be a wonderful father. I would like to thank Barry Clark for all of his help with the *Love That Lasts* workshop series. I would like to thank Diane Kort for listening to all of my ideas over the years. I would like to acknowledge Hedley and Emily for their example of a loving and fun partnership. A big thank you to Sherrie Beyer for all of her enthusiasm about my work. Thank you very much Sheryl Goodspeed for your illustrations. Thank you Anthony for all of your work on my book cover. Lastly, thank you to PublishAmerica for publishing my book!

Contents

Part I
Chapter 1 - Love 11
Chapter 2 - Choosing a Partner 15
Chapter 3 - Building a Fulfilling Relationship 19
Chapter 4 - Pitfalls 27
Chapter 5 - Relationship Tools 31
Chapter 6 - Finding Help 39
Chapter 7 - Entering Relationships with Kids 43

Part II
Chapter 8 - One 47
Chapter 9 - Transformative Love 51
Chapter 10 - Self Love 53
Chapter 11 - Relationships that End 55
Chapter 12 - True Healing 63

Part I

Chapter 1
Love

What is Love?

The world's great wisdom traditions say that love is the ultimate reality of existence. In human romantic relationships, the more we strive to reflect that divine, universal love, the more harmony and freedom we will have with our partner. Real love has no agendas, no attachments, no ideas, no demands, and no conditions. These are all things we add to the experience of love, which begin to contaminate our love, and which also begin to confuse us about what love is. Real, uncontaminated love has one simple agenda: to love!

Our minds can talk about love, but they can't actually experience love. Love can only be experienced through feeling. Many times we confuse the experience of love with the word or idea of love. You can say the words "I love you," and not be feeling love. You can also feel love when you think you can't or shouldn't.

True love of another human being wants what is best for them even if that's not you. Our idea of what is best for them and what is truly best for them may be different.

Real love can't be used as a "bargaining chip." (Example: "I will love you if you promise to never leave or hurt me.") Bargaining and other forms of manipulation begin to contaminate our love for another human being.

What Gets in the Way of Love?

Eclipsed Love
When fear and neediness begin to contaminate our love, we begin to see our partner as being responsible for fulfilling our present needs and our unfulfilled childhood needs. We become clingy, jealous, petty and overly critical.

The following statements represent contaminated and confused love:
I'll love you if _____
If you really loved me you would _____
If you loved me you wouldn't _____
If you love me how can you _____
You don't really love because _____
You owe me because I love you.
If you love me how can you leave me?

Note: Two people can absolutely love each other and still not be good company or partners in a relationship for one another. You don't have to stop loving someone to leave a relationship. You can simply leave because it's not right for you. Real love is clean and pure. If you want to be happy, keep it distinct from your needs and desires. They can be addressed openly and honestly without using love as a manipulation tactic.

Withholding Love
The "Withholding Love Game" often starts between parents and kids. Parents withhold their love when they are not pleased with their child. Over the course of raising the child they withhold their love many times to discipline and control the child. The child wants to win back Mommy and Daddy's love and tries to change to please Mommy and Daddy, beginning their conditioning that they have to win or deserve love. When

children raised this way are mad at Mommy and Daddy they also eventually learn to punish them by withholding their love.

As children we are dependent on our parents for our survival. We are also much smaller than them and not on an even playing field. So we really don't have much of a choice as to whether we participate in the "Withholding Love Game."

The problem is that when we grow up, we never stop playing these games. We continue to withhold love in our relationships to control and to punish, a damaging game which is very destructive to building happy relationships. We also lose individually, because love is a force that is greater than us, and when we block that force we damage ourselves more than anybody else. Withheld love begins to destroy us internally. Next time you are withholding love, notice how it makes you feel—usually kind of icky or sick!

Note for anyone who has ever had their heart broken: Many of us assume that the way to get over a broken heart is to stop loving the other person, or withhold our love from them. From my experience, loving the person more, while at the same time starting to let go of our attachment to what role they are supposed to play in our life, is the way out of a broken heart. It is still going to hurt, but you won't be fighting inside yourself and trying to pretend you don't love them. The healing comes much quicker with the surrender of loving and letting go of attachment.

Chapter 2
Choosing a Partner

Choosing a partner wisely is a very important step to creating a fulfilling relationship. Relationships are so easy to get into, and can be so complicated and painful to get out of. You don't want to rush this step! Even if you are already in a relationship, you may find these useful. In many cases awareness of these keys can improve a current relationship.

Many times out of desperation and loneliness we project our fantasies onto another human being, only to discover later that they are nothing like we were imagining. Important: Be willing to take the time to get to know who the person really is rather than projecting your fantasy of who they are. A good relationship needs to be grounded in reality, not in fantasy.

While I can't tell anyone exactly how to choose a partner who is right for them, I have found certain keys to be a good guide.

Key #1: Best Friend/Companion

If you are going to take the journey through this life with a partner, it's just common sense to pick a person who you can be best friends with. Remember what it was like to have a best friend when you were a kid? That is what you are looking for in a partner—someone you simply enjoy spending time with.

Key #2: Same Team

A relationship is a team. Some problems arise because we've chosen someone who's a "bad teammate," or maybe we ourselves are bad teammates. I recommend choosing a partner who is interested in playing on the same team as you! Some people are going to have to grow and struggle quite a bit to make good teammates. If you think you haven't been a good teammate, it's not too late to change.

Key #3: Feeling Safe and at Ease

If you find someone with whom you feel really at ease, and with whom you can just be yourself, that's a really good sign. If you are choosing a partner, it's just common sense to be with someone who makes you feel relaxed and comfortable. This is a very important indicator of a potentially happy relationship.

Key #4: Behind the Scenes

When it's just the two of you, what does it feel like? Ultimately, you are going to spend a lot of time alone with this person. Make sure that you are picking someone who is fun for you to be with alone. This is something that no one else can tell you. Only the two of you know what it's really like "behind the scenes."

Key #5: Kindness

I recommend looking for a partner who is kind, gentle and loving, not just towards you, but also towards people in general. Someone who's kind to you, but unkind to others may just be temporarily on his/her best behavior to try and win your love.

Key #6: Someone Who Loves You 100%

Don't settle for less. You deserve someone who loves you passionately, "all-out." Watch out for ambivalent people and trying to win their love. Also, be fair to the other person: pick someone who you are passionately in love with. It's only magic if you have two people who are loving each other 100% and feel lucky to have each other.

Key #7: Honesty/Willingness to Work at It
Honesty is critical to maintaining a good relationship. Pick someone who you feel is honest with you and that you feel comfortable being honest with. It's also important to pick a partner who is willing to work on the relationship. Almost all relationships have some problems from time to time.

Four Things to Watch Out For:

1)Falling in Love with Potential. This is a very dangerous game. It is wonderful to see potential in other people. Yet, if you aren't happy with the way they are right now, don't make a commitment based on who you hope they become someday. That day may never happen, or take much longer than you could imagine. It's not fair to you or to them.

2) Excitement/Strong Physical Attraction. Of course, there is nothing wrong with strong physical attraction as such. Often, however, because of the euphoria and excitement, we fail to really get to know the person as a person, choosing to stay dreamy about them because it feels so good-that is, until months or years later when the euphoria wears off and we discover we don't really know them. It's fine to be really drawn to someone; just be willing to put it on the side so you can also really see them and find out who they are.

3) Physical or Verbal Abuse. Physical and verbal abuse rarely get better with time. Usually they get worse and escalate with time. It is possible to get mad at your partner and express the anger cleanly without being verbally abusive or mean. (Again: I highly recommend picking someone who is kind!)

4) One Way Street. No matter how great you think he/she is, if he/she doesn't reciprocate your adoration, it's best to move on. You deserve someone who adores and loves you 100%. I know this can be challenging, particularly if you really think this person could be great for you. Many times we stay hoping to win their love or that one day they will turn around and love us the way we are loving them if they just get to know us. Don't spend too much time with someone who isn't really into you. Somewhere there may be someone whom you love and who adores you too—where you could have love coming from both sides of the street.

Chapter 3
Building a Fulfilling Relationship

What Is a Relationship?

In some ways, "relationship" is a made-up concept. A relationship can be created any way that works for the two people involved. Often we get fixated on past images of what a relationship is supposed to look like: parents, movies, fantasies, and even previous relationships. Many times we limit our enjoyment by holding on to our attachments of what we think a relationship is supposed to look like.

The more exciting possibility is to invent whatever relationship would work best for the two people involved. There is really no specific way a relationship has to look. It can be a truly exciting art to sit down with another human being and invent a relationship that will mutually support both of you. This also keeps the door open to recreating the relationship or aspects of the relationship from time to time so both people will continue to be served and enlivened.

Note: Even if you have been in a relationship for many years, you can still recreate or add more to your existing relationship as long as both people are committed to having a fulfilling relationship.

Warning: It's important that both people authentically want to be in the relationship. If one partner is secretly ambivalent, or staying because they are scared to leave, that person will tend to unconsciously sabotage any effort to create a healthy relationship.

Understanding Your Partner

Getting to know one's partner can be a life-long fascination. Just as there is no end to what human beings can discover in themselves, there's no end to what you can experience in the discovery of another human being. One of the keys to staying in love is developing a fascination and curiosity about your partner and to engage in the fun of watching their life unfold. Many relationships go stale when partners put each other in boxes, force unnecessary restrictions on each other, and lastly, try to mold their partner in the image they think is right.

Different Machines

Every human being has their own type of "inner machinery." Many of us make the mistake of relating and reacting to other human beings as though their machinery was exactly the same as ours. Although we all share vast similarities, we also have different inner workings and nuances. Many times what seems obvious to us is completely invisible to our partner. It's okay that they don't see it the same way. Take the time to get to know your partner's machinery.

Many of our conflicts are simply misunderstandings and misinterpretations around what was said and meant. Two different machines can interpret the same thing in two completely different ways. For example: have you ever been really upset about what you thought someone said, only to find out later what you thought they were saying wasn't what they meant? The same words being said from one person to another can be interpreted in a totally different way than the speaker meant.

Loving All-Out

To have any chance of something really special with another human being, it's essential to transcend the pettiness of possession and neediness. Be willing to love beyond getting what you want. Make your priority be loving the person and wanting what's best for them, even if it's not you at some point. This doesn't make you a sucker. You can love your partner all out and still choose to leave the relationship if they don't treat you well. This is, in fact, loving yourself all out (which is also essential to having a good relationship with another human being).

Many times what keeps people from having a good relationship is their fear of losing one another. **Important:** It's critical to make the love and the friendship of another human being senior to the relationship. If not, the relationship becomes more important to you than the other person or their happiness. To have a transcendent relationship, your attachment to the relationship needs to be secondary to your commitment to love and support one another whether or not you stay together. I know it is ironic, but this road actually gives you the possibility of a wonderful life-long partnership. The other road keeps you in fear and desperation.

Right or Happy

The majority of us would like to be right and happy. So why choose? Well, usually when we are right, someone else is wrong. This is particularly damaging in your relationship. If you are right (win) then your partner is wrong (lose). Look for win-win situations; be willing for both of you to be some right and some wrong. More importantly, ask yourself: how can we resolve this issue so that it works for both of us and we can get back to loving each other? Again, it's caring more about the team than the empty ego gratification of being right alone. Being right is a bad trade for love.

Taking Responsibility
We all have our moments of being a real jerk or jerkette. When you realize that you have been acting like a jerk, own up and say you're sorry. In apologizing you may also be able to learn from the experience and become aware of how to be a jerk less of the time in life.

Communication
Many couples, for a variety of reasons, stop talking. Keeping communication open is critical for a successful relationship. Planning regular weekly times to sit down and talk is a good idea. Allow both parties to express anything they may need to say. **Note:** Remember to be a good listener!

Learning How to Listen
Most of us have no idea how terrible we are at listening. We assume we are listening when another human being is talking, while most of the time we are thinking, evaluating, judging or associating.

The Interpretation Box: We all have one of these. While another person is speaking we are thinking, judging, associating or evaluating (which is not listening). I agree or I disagree, right or wrong, should or shouldn't, good or bad, I like you or I don't like you, what am I going to say next or this reminds me of the time, etc. The bad news is there is no "on and off switch" for the interpretation box. The good news is once you recognize that you have an interpretation box in your head, then you can make a choice to put aside your interpretation box and really hear the other person. To choose to really hear the person talking to you over your ideas, judgments, and evaluations can open new doors in intimacy and connecting with another human being. This feels far superior to being critical or analytical, not to mention that being really heard is a huge gift to the speaker.

Good therapists know that the key to assisting their clients in healing is largely in the quality of their listening.

To become a good listener is a life-long practice and discipline. When another human being is speaking, practice putting your full attention on them rather than on what you are thinking. Give them 100% of your attention and practice listening to them with your entire being (eyes, ears, mind, body, feeling body, and soul).

Don't interrupt the speaker! When you interrupt you are unconsciously saying that you have no respect for them or what they have to say, which many times will lead them not to respect what you have to say. Often this is when disagreements turn into fights that start to get mean and ugly.

I realize, present company included, that the majority of us interrupt the speaker from time to time. I would recommend when you notice yourself interrupting the speaker that you stop yourself in mid-sentence, and say, "I am sorry I just realized I interrupted you and I want to hear what you have to say." This practice will begin to train you to be a better listener and interrupt less.

Honesty and Openness

It goes almost without saying that you need to be honest to have a good relationship. Sometimes people feel like they are being honest because they haven't told any outright lies, but at the same time they aren't being very open with sharing their feelings, vulnerability, or whatever else maybe happening inside them. For someone to have a chance to get really close to you, it is essential to allow them to get beyond your surface walls. This allows the relationship to connect on deeper and more intimate levels. It also means allowing yourself to be vulnerable. This is a very important point: be gentle to your partner when they are vulnerable. If you are mean or critical they will be much less likely to let you in again.

How Do You Create More Honesty and Openness in Your Relationship?

For starters, have the courage to be more open and honest yourself. From my personal experience, when you become more open and honest, most people will respond by becoming more open and honest back. It's kind of like everyone is waiting for the other person to go first.

Again, listening: how you listen matters. If you create a space with your listening that feels safe to your partner, he/she is likely to be more open with you. Over time as we discover that someone is a safe person to open up and express our real selves with, we will continue to open up.

Underneath our facades and layers of armor, we all are these beautiful vulnerable beings, like sweet children. The reason we developed the armor in the first place was to protect that soft and innocent part of ourselves from attacks. It takes time to trust if we let down our masks and armor that we won't be punched in the stomach. So, if you want your partner to be more open with you, be sensitive and gentle when they are opening up. If you are mean and critical when they are being open, they will be far less likely to open up again.

Ultimately: The place to get is where both of you can drop your masks and armor with each other. Then you can simply just be yourselves with one another. That in itself is one of the greatest gifts of being in a good relationship!

Sex

Most of us over-complicate this area. Sex is an important part of a fulfilling relationship, but it's far from the most important component. We also can use it as a drug addict uses a drug as an escape from our problems.

Only have sex if both partners want to have sex. Each partner should be responsible for their own sexual needs. If you want sex and your partner doesn't, don't try to talk them into it; rather, be willing to be responsible for your own sexually needs and take care of them yourself (masturbation). This way the sex doesn't become a burden for either partner. Instead you keep the sex sacred by only having sex when both partners are into it.

Don't be a selfish lover! When you both decide that you want to have sex, be sensitive enough to make sure that both partners have a good time.

Note: For many people, desire is not as much about being attracted as it is feeling emotionally connected (especially true in longer term relationships). Often when a partner says that they aren't physically attracted to their partner any more, often the truth is they aren't feeling emotionally connected with their partner. If you or your partner are not feeling sexually interested in each other, this is often an indicator of being emotionally disconnected and probably needing to express the anger and hurt feelings that are blocking the deeper feelings of love for each other.

Remembering to Have Fun

Most couples do a good job of having fun for the first few months, or even years of their relationship. Then many times they stop having fun together. I guess between kids, work, and life's obligations they can't find the time. If you find this happening to you, it's a good idea to plan something fun at least once a week that the two of you can do alone. If you have kids, it may be getting a babysitter just so the two of you can have a relaxing evening at home alone. Playing and having fun is one of the primary ways that human beings bond! If you stop having fun together a relationship will often go stale or feel flat.

Playing on the Same Team

Do you play on the same team as your partner?
If you see your partner as being on your team, when you have a conflict it becomes a challenge for you to work to resolve (the conflict is outside the relationship).

If you see your partner as your opponent, then the conflict is you against your partner. The conflict then often becomes a war about winning rather than about resolution.

It is possible to create a relationship based on team playing where each partner is engaged in contribution to the other. Choosing to play consciously together as a team shifts the focus from individual needs to the larger needs of the relationship as a whole. When this happens, there is an increase in the intimacy, openness and love available.

On the individual level, when you are working with each other, as opposed to working against each other, you may discover that many aspects of your life will be elevated.

Final thought: Most couples are provided with the opportunity either to elevate each other's lives for the better or wreak havoc in each other's lives.

Best Friends

It takes time, work, and trust to build this kind of friendship, where you can drop your masks and armor with each other. Then you can just simply be yourselves with one another, and that is a special and rare place in this world.

Chapter 4
Pitfalls

Unexpressed Anger/Hurt Feelings

Over time, withheld anger and hurt feelings cover up our ability to feel our love for another human being. Part of being honest is expressing to your partner what you are mad or hurt about (without being mean or abusive). Conversely, be willing to allow your partner to share their feelings of anger and hurt with you. I know it can be challenging to listen to at times. Yet, in any relationship feelings are going to get hurt and people are going to get mad. The ability to express and listen to hurt feelings and anger and get over them is critical to having a long-term fulfilling relationship. I know expressing anger and hurt feelings can sometimes be taboo in our culture. But people can get over being hurt or mad, it's far from the end of the world. In fact, once you have experienced staying with another human being while they are hurt or mad at you, and eventually getting to the other side, you will discover that this can be quite a gift to your relationship. In fact, you are likely to experience a new level of intimacy and love in your relationship. Since this is an area that many of us have never been taught how to deal with, it may be best to find a skilled mediator, counselor, or therapist for the first time, particularly for coaching in how to keep your anger clean and non-abusive. Lastly, remember the idea of expressing your anger or hurt feelings is to get over them, not to punish, blame or belittle your partner.

When expressing anger, keep it simple. Leave your story and blame out! Say, "I am mad at you for what you said or did." Be specific; don't add extra venom. Again, the idea isn't to punish the other person, but to get over your anger/hurt so you can love them again.

Again, this is probably something that you will not be able to get fully by reading and applying. I recommend getting some help/training for at least the first few times.

Falling Asleep

Many times as we fall into routines with our significant other, somewhere between "pass the coffee," and "I'm late to work," we stop making real contact with our partner. One day we fall asleep and the next thing we know, years have passed and we wake up wondering what happened? How did we lose sight of each other? One of the pitfalls for all human beings is that we tend to go unconscious with anything that is routine in our life, including our partner. No matter how wonderful they may be, given time, we tend to take our loved ones for granted. Don't forget to love the people in your life every day! This world is full of tales of people who only when faced with the loss of a loved one discovered how much more they wish they had expressed. Make the people in your life the priority, not the other stuff! If you have ever lost a loved one, you understood instantly that all that other stuff wasn't really all that important at all. Make it your priority every day to love the people in your life all out. This will help you guard against falling asleep and taking each other for granted.

We don't have as much time in this life as we may think, and you never know when it's the last time you will see a loved one. I recommend loving with a sense of urgency and not taking your time with a significant other for granted! I say this not to scare you, but to wake you up; we all can use a reminder from time to time.

Drama

Much of our art and entertainment is about drama. Most of us learned our relationship style from a combination of art and entertainment and our experience of our parents and other significant adults who we saw in relationship as we were growing up. Many of us feel that relationships are about drama, which is what much of our entertainment suggests. Many of us are also addicted to drama. The intensity makes us feel more alive.

It's true that any relationship is likely to have at least a little drama on occasion. Unfortunately, in many relationships the drama never stops. Life will bring problems and challenges to any relationship, but the challenges are much easier to work through if we don't add extra juice to them by overdramatizing them. We often make a much bigger deal of these problems than necessary. Then we get other outside people (family, friends, etc.) enrolled in our drama. After all, a good drama needs more than two characters!

The cost is happiness. While we are living in the drama (which has a certain level of excitement) we are not likely to resolve our problems and challenges. Instead, we are more likely to keep the drama going. The focus is on the drama, not on resolving the problem: this is the real problem with drama…it's a distraction from dealing with the real problems and challenges. Moreover, it adds layers of confusion and distance between ourselves and our partners.

Note: Real love expressed and shared is far more enlivening then any drama we create.

Ground Hog Day (Repeat Fights)

Unresolved conflicts tend to repeat themselves. Many times couples have been having the same fight for over twenty years and don't even realize it because the content is slightly different, but at its root the problem is coming from the same place. If you find yourself in that same déjà vu pattern, get help: it will save you a lot of unnecessary pain in the future.

Blame

The closest of teams will lose unity under the destructive force of blaming. If your relationship is having problems, it's both people's fault. Many times one or both partners blame the other person for all the difficulties in their relationship. This destroys the couple's unity, making them opponents rather than teammates. Your life is 100% your responsibility. If it's not working out the way you think it should, it's not your partner's fault. Blame is a waste of time game that alienates and distracts from improving conditions. Blame becomes your action. If you look for solutions rather than blame, you have the opportunity to improve conditions.

Lack of Respect *"You can be mad and respectful"*

Many couples come to me after they have been mean and disrespectful, or outright nasty to one another. It takes so much longer to untangle all the hurt feeling and built-up anger once couples have started being mean to each other. Usually the actual issue isn't that hard to resolve. You can be mad at your partner without being mean or disrespectful. Once the mean game starts it usually continues to escalate to more and more destructive levels. Respect isn't a feeling; it's a choice about how to treat someone regardless of our feelings. Please don't be mean to each other. If you have been being mean, stop! Get help if you don't know how.

Chapter 5
Relationship Tools

If you would like to begin to improve your relationship and you are not sure where to begin, these exercises may be of assistance. As is the case with most things, consistency is important!

1) Pen Exercise (Talking piece)
Have both partners sit facing each other, in a quiet comfortable setting. Turn off the phone and make sure you won't be interrupted for at least a half an hour. Partners take turns sharing, with each partner speaking for a minimum of fifteen minutes. Don't interrupt the person speaking. The person holding the pen talks while the other person listens. The job of the person listening is to practice listening outside their "Interpretation box" (see Chapter 3). After the person holding the pen is finished talking, the other person takes the pen and it's their turn to talk while their partner practices listening.

Note: Make sure that each partner speaks for a minimum of fifteen minutes. If it's been less then fifteen minutes, stay silent until the person with the pen can think of more stuff to share. This exercise also helps partners get better at sharing about their lives with one another.
Do this exercise every night for at least thirty days.

Features: Very good for improving the quality of your listening in your relationship. Begins to give partners a better understanding of how to listen to one another without interrupting. Often improves the quality of open communication and sharing.

2) The Contribution Game

This is the best tool in my box. This exercise has the power not only to transform your relationship, but your life as well. You must do it from a place of love and service, and throw your whole self into it with reckless abandon.

How to play: Both you and your partner pick one day each to serve the other partner. For example, Monday could be my day to serve my partner, and Saturday could be my partner's day to serve me. If you are too busy, give at least half a day each way to serve one another with no other work obligations.

The game is simple. On your partner's day, do anything they ask. They may want you to do work or cooking for them, snuggle them, massage them, and on and on. If you are being served, ask for whatever you want or need. If you want your partner to listen to you, ask for that. If you want your partner to go somewhere with you, ask for that. It's very important to ask for what you want. Warning: don't abuse your partner on the day they are serving you. This is an exercise in love and service, not cruelty and punishment.

Play the game for at least six months consistently.

Benefits: Too many to list!

When Serving: Really get into the role of serving your partner. I found my serving days to be some of the best days of my life.

When Being Served: Feel free to ask for whatever you want. This is how you partner will begin to understand you better.

3) Weekly Fun

Many couples stop making the time to have fun together. Plan something once a week that both you and your partner can do together that is fun for both of you.

I recommend you play this game for a minimum of three months, but really you should do it for life.

Note: Mystery dates can be fun!

Benefits: having fun together continues to breathe life into your relationship and helps you continue to deepen your bond.

4) Weekly Conversation

Plan a time every week that you can get together and talk. Remember to be a good listener. Use the pen exercise if you need it.

Have at least a couple hours available. If it works for you, it may be nice to start with a shared meditation or prayer.

Benefits: Helps keep communication open and you in touch with one another.

5) What to Do When Stuck

Writing Exercise. Have both people write down everything that is important to them, and that they are bothered by, regarding the issue needing resolution. Have one person read first, while the other listens. Important: don't interrupt! Then have the second person read while their partner listens. After both are done reading, ask questions and see if you can discuss some possible solutions. Or, have both people go back to writing up some possible solutions. If needed, use a neutral third party to help mediate during this exercise.

Time Out. If you find yourself in a conflict that has become unproductive, mean, and mostly about anger, call a time-out and come back to resolve when both parties have calmed down.

Get Help. If you find that you are not able to resolve the conflict internally, find someone who can help you resolve the conflict and get back to loving each other. This can be a therapist, a mediator, a priest, a coach, or just a wise friend whom you both trust. You may have to try a few people to find one that works for both of you.

6) Couples Questionnaire: Nine Questions to help you gain insight into your relationship

1) Background: How long have you been in your relationship? What have you liked? Not liked?

2) What period was the best time in your relationship? Why?

3) What period has been the worst in your relationship? Why?

4) What are you angry at your partner about?

5) Do you have things that you feel hurt about from the past with your partner?

6) What do you feel grateful to your partner for?

7) What do you think are the main issues in your relationship?

TRANSFORMATIVE LOVE
A Healing Guide to Intimate Relationships

8) How would you like your relationship to be?

9) What are some things you have done in your relationship that you may feel bad or guilty about?

7) Couples Rooms of Life Questionnaire - Questions to help yourself and your partner see the big picture and how your life or lives maybe affecting your relationship.

Please answer the following 5 questions for each of the 9 rooms of life below:
1) How is this area of your life going?
2) Are you happy (content) with this area?
3) What would you like to improve about this area?
4) What are some actions you could take to improve this area?
5) What stops you from improving this area? What are your favorite excuses?

Rooms of Life:
1) Work
2) Money
3) Family
4) Social Life
5) Love Relationship
6) Health & Exercise
7) Spiritual Life
8) Home
9) Fun (activities of interest)

8) EVIL Partner Exercise

Write up: In story form
Everything you are *mad* about, *resentful* about, *hurt* about, *imagine* about, *don't like* about, *don't trust* about, *think is mean*

about, and *think is manipulative* about your partner, and everything that has been *frustrating* about your relationship. Lastly, write up how wonderful you have been despite all of this terribleness you have endured from your partner (ham this part up!)

At the end of story go back and read everything you have written and then:

List the big three things you are hurt about or resentful about towards your partner.

Then Write up (again in story form)
What a monster you are and how terrible you are to your partner. Play up and exaggerate! Really make yourself sound terrible in regards to your partner (Bonus for humor)

At the end of the story go back and read everything you have written and then:

List the three things you regret most that you have done

Next write up what you have learned from this exercise and what insights you have discovered about your self and relationship.

Lastly, write up what you appreciate about your partner and what you appreciate about your relationship.

This is an exercise that you and your partner can share with each other. It may be necessary to have a counselor or wise friend to help you work through some of the hurt or resentment.
Some of the benefits: Clarity, potential healing, letting go of stories, and many more.

9) Conflict and Relationship Exercise

Instructions:

On a separate sheet of paper, please list all the significant relationships you have had in your life. Parents, family, close friends, lovers, teachers, etc. (minimum of twenty) Note: The people don't have to be alive (a deceased grandparent very much counts)

Now go back and give each person a number from 1 to 10. — 1 being you can't stand them! And them living on the same planet is to close. 10 being you feel absolutely great about them and would welcome a visit at anytime.

Now go back, and with the people six or below, write down what some of the conflicts or issues are that you have with them.

Lastly, are some of the conflicts or issues repetitive? Do they come up in your current relationships? In your marriage or with your romantic partner? With people you work with? Or in your social life?

What I have found is that every relationship affects every other relationship in our life. If we have unresolved issues with our mother, they will tend to play out unconsciously in our current relationship or at our work or in our social life.

Most of the couples I have worked with in conflict are acting out conflicts that are not just about the present situation, but also about unfinished conflicts from their past in their respective lives.

Example:
1) Mom—8
2) Dad—7
3) Amy (girlfriend)—9
4) Sally (friend)—4

Chapter 6
Finding Help

When it comes to getting help there are a lot of resources out there: Therapists, Mediators, Life Coaches, Spiritual teachers, Personal growth workshops, and Couples Retreats, to name a few. If you decide to do couples counseling, I would recommend sessions that are at least two hours long. If the counselor's sessions are normally one hour, ask to schedule for two hours instead. I would also recommend someone that gives weekly assignments and exercises for you to practice in your life.

Warning: It may take several or more attempts to find someone that is the right counselor, coach or other for you and your partner. I would recommend someone you both like, feel comfortable with and of course is making a difference.

Obstacles: I think the two biggest obstacles to finding help are: 1) Not knowing you need help, and 2) Shame about getting help.

Not knowing you need help
Sometimes it can be hard to see from inside the relationship that you need help, or you may think this is just how life is, or everyone has problems, or this really isn't that bad. It is usually not what we know about life that is the problem, but rather what we have no idea about that is the problem. For example: When

I used to lead Domestic Violence Counseling groups, often new members would tell me that they weren't angry. It wasn't until much later in the process that they would look back and say, "Wow, I was really angry." The problem wasn't that they were liars. It was more likely that they had been angry for so long that it felt normal. Sometimes we don't realize that life could be much better than what we are used to settling for.

Shame about getting help
A wise person knows when to ask for help!

It is unfortunate that getting help can be looked upon as a personal failing. I would imagine that most couples would need at least a little help at some point in their relationship.

I think that creating a fulfilling, passionate, and alive long-term relationship would be at least equally as challenging as becoming a professional athlete. Yet, professional athletes have coaches and trainers to help them maximize their ability. I have never heard a top athlete say I don't need any help; I just want to do this on my own.

There are a couple of reason why most people can't solve all their problems in a relationship: 1) They haven't been taught how (it would be like saying I don't know how to fly a plane but I don't need any training). Most people haven't been taught the skills to express resentment and hurt cleanly and get over it. Therefore, most people in relationships remain stuck in resentment and hurt which can block their ability to feel love for each other. 2) Nobody is that wise when it comes to themselves, particularly in conflict. Often we are unable to see our own blind spots and how we are tangled up with our partner. This is where an outside person can be of great assistance.

Final thought: I am all for people being able to work through things themselves, and my question would be, how much time do you give yourself? For example, if you say we can handle this ourselves I would recommend coming up with a plan on how you are going to work through this issue and give yourselves an amount of time to do so (say two weeks or a month). If you were not able to work through this issue by this designated time, then I would recommend getting some help.

Chapter 7
Entering Relationships with Kids

I have added this chapter into this book because I am aware of the growing numbers of divorces, single parents, and step parents out there in the world today. And my strong desire for the children of this world is to get more Love!

Step parents
We do not have a shortage of children on this earth; in fact we have a surplus in ratio to good parents. These days, many children have only one parent raising them. Often this is their mom. Many times their biological fathers are missing for one reason or another. This leaves a huge and unique role open for step parents. Believe me when I say this child needs you to love them. Even if your stepchild has two active parents in her life, you are still very much needed by the child.

If you have decided to partner with a woman or man who has children, you have chosen to be part of a family. Many times, because of lack of maturity, we don't see this obvious fact. We may think we are marrying our partner, not the children. In reality, to have a successful marriage with the person you love, their kids are a big part of the package. You are really signing up to be a part of a family and subbing in for a missing part of that family.

For our society to evolve to a better place, we need more people to see this opportunity and take on the missing roles in the lives of children. The worst way to handle this opportunity is to go into it half-hearted. I would recommend either choosing to play a big part in the children's life or don't choose to be with a person who has children.

Part II

Chapter 8
One

The following story represents the forgotten truth that keeps us separated from love in our lives. Note: Transformative Love exists in the unity of oneness, and conditional love exists in the separation of self and others, which can lead to manipulative and lonely relationships.

There was once a little girl who lived in a village...
As she began to grow older, she started to become aware that people in the village hurt each other. She became very depressed about all the pain she witnessed happening in her village. She could not understand why the people of her village would hurt each other. She decided to leave the village in search of answers. She began her walk into the unknown forest. She soon came across a bear.

She asked, "Mr. Bear, why do the people of my village hurt each other?"

Mr. Bear answered, "I am not old or wise enough to know why your people hurt each other. I have not been here very long, and all I've known of your people is that they needlessly hurt each other. Perhaps you could ask the trees, the older ones have been here for 200 years. Maybe they could tell you why your people hurt each other."

The little girl thanked the bear and continued on her journey through the forest. Later that day, she came upon a giant tree that looked like it must be the oldest tree in the forest.

She asked, "Mr. Tree, why do the people of my village hurt each other?"

The tree answered, "I have been here a long time and have seen many animals come and go, including the people of your village. They are the only animal I've seen that hurt each other, as well as my fellow trees and many of the other animals for no reason. It has been puzzling to me, and I am sorry that I cannot answer your question. Perhaps the minerals will know. They have been here far longer than I have."

The little girl thanked the tree and continued on her journey through the forest. She soon discovered a great big rock in her path. At this point, her little legs had become quite tired from all of her walking.

She gratefully sat on top of the big rock, and then she asked, "Mr. Rock, do you know why the people of my village hurt each other?"

The rock answered, "I have seen many things in my time here. I have seen people come and go, and I remember when the people of your village settled here. At one time human beings didn't hurt each other. They now hurt each other because they have forgotten."

The little girl asked, "What have they forgotten?"

The rock responded, "They have forgotten that we are all one. The people, the trees, the animals and the minerals are all one. And when the human beings forgot that we are all one, the separation they felt inside was so painful that they began to lash out and do harm to each other and the rest of the world."

The little girl asked, "If I go back to my village and tell my people this, will they stop hurting each other?"

The rock responded, "Probably not — it will not be from their minds that they will remember that they are one. It will need to be communicated to their hearts."

The little girl asked, "What can I do then?"

The rock answered, "People will remember when they are ready to remember. You will know what to do when you return to your village."

The little girl thanked the rock and continued on her way. She returned to the village later that day, and as she listened to her heart, she began to sing a beautiful song. As she sang, some of the people in *her village who were ready began to remember that we are all one. As she sang and others joined her as the days passed, more and more people of her village started to remember that we are all one.*

That little child continues to be born in this world.
She is born in each of us, and you will see her when you are ready to remember "that we are all one."

Chapter 9
Transformative Love

Our soul's deepest desire is to fall in love with the entire world and everything in it.

Transformative love is love for everyone and everything in this world. To remember the interconnectedness of all life. Many times we think that we can pick and choose whom we treat kindly. We will be loving and kind to our partner, and judgmental, critical and cold to people we don't like. I am not suggesting that you would be best friends and close with everyone. Yet, if you pay attention you will see that sometimes you will be critical and cold to your partner. The way we are BEING in life tends to transfer from one situation to the next and affect all of our relationships. If we are judgmental and critical of others, we will be judgmental and critical of ourselves and anyone else in our life. When we become more accepting of other people's imperfection, we also become more accepting of our own imperfection.

The more you love in life, the more you will love in your relationship. Our soul's deepest desire is to fall in love with the entire world and everything in it. I realize for most of us (myself included) this is very much an on-going journey. This is the journey that transforms our contaminated love (full of conditions and limitations) to Divine and pure love. As I write this I am aware that I fall far short of this mission most of the time and every once in a while I have a day where I wake up and I feel love for everybody and everything in this world. These days are the most magnificent days of my life. I feel so alive and connected, and a part of everything. I feel a deep sense of contentment, clarity, and belonging.

Most of us think we need to be loved to be happy. I disagree I think we need to love to be happy and the more we love the happier we are. People sometimes say, how can you love this person because they have hurt people? I can love the person and dislike or even hate their actions. Many people will think that they will be weak or taken advantage of if they love. I would say they don't understand love or their greater nature. Love is the most powerful force in this universe. I can love someone and at the same time be mad at them for their actions. In fact, I would say I need to get mad at most of the people in my life from time to time and get over it with them so I can get back to feeling the love that I have them. Being loving doesn't mean that I will walk on eggshells and be careful not to offend you. It means that I am willing to risk being deeply honest with you and willing to work through whatever might come up between us because I am committed to loving you.

Final thought: Our true nature is to love. It simply feels good when we are loving. The more you are able to transform with love and honesty your relationships with family, friends, colleagues, strangers, trees, and the entire world, the more loving your romantic partnership will be. Every relationship we have affects every other relationship we have.

Chapter 10
Self Love

You don't need to learn how to love yourself because you already do.

I imagine that self-love is a critical aspect of building a fulfilling relationship with another human being. This is something we can also work on whether we are single or in a relationship.

I will confess, that I don't always love myself. I would say that most of the time I really like myself a lot and feel loving towards myself, and I also have quite a few moments when I am hard on myself and I am not particularly kind to myself.

Over the years I have reflected a lot on the words "self love." In my late teens and early twenties, when I was going through some depressing times, these words were said to me quite often, "You need to learn how to love yourself." I would think "that sounds like a good idea, but how do I do that?" I didn't seem to get very useful answers about how to love myself. I am not even entirely sure I will be able to come up with a useful answer now for how to love yourself. I would however, like to share some of my experience on this journey.

I first suggest that you don't need to learn how to love yourself because you already do. One of the things I have discovered over time in my meditation and prayer practice, is that I have a compassionate observer inside of me that watches all the other parts and the drama they regularly create. What I have learned is that this compassionate observer loves me very much and has always been loving me. I just didn't notice for the longest time because I identified myself more with the critical and louder voices in my head. I allowed them to distract me from knowing the compassionate observer that lived inside of me. I am also sure that this compassionate observer lives in all of us. I think back to my teenage years, and it would have been helpful for me to know that there is a part of me that was already loving me, and that part was more of who I really was than the thoughts and ideas that I was identifying as me. I think the way to self love is to rediscover the compassionate observer living inside of us and to realize that this part of ourselves has never stopped loving us.

Final thought: Our capacity to identify ourselves with the compassionate observer is directly related to our ability to love ourselves and love other people.

Chapter 11
Relationships that End

End of relationship, Broken Heart, and Being single.

End of relationship

Everything is an opportunity for something beautiful to emerge even when a relationship is ending.

In my humblest opinion, we come into relationships to grow and evolve. Not all relationships will span the course of our life. For most of us, we have some experience with relationships ending. A relationship ending can be a very traumatic event. In many cases, it is the death of a dream of happily ever after. Many people think that if the relationship isn't going to work, then it doesn't matter how it ends. I would highly caution against this philosophy. I would say often how you end a relationship sets you up for how you will start your next relationship and what baggage will be carried over from the previous relationship to be worked though in your new relationship. I would also like to suggest that there is no such thing as the end of a relationship. The end of the romantic partnership is not an ending of your relationship, but rather a transformation of the relationship to something else. That something else is the opportunity that is often missed. Often people separate and remain angry at one another for years or longer. And I ask, if you are angry and bitter at someone else, who gets to feel that anger every time you are reminded of him or her? Yes, of course you! That is right. The anger and unresolved feelings live in you. As the divorce rate continues to climb, I would like to see a commitment added to the marriage agreements that if one or both of us decides to leave, we will first continue to work things out between us with the hope that we can leave with a feeling of completion and an understanding of what we had to learn from each other and the relationship. You don't have to stay in the relationship while you are doing this; you just have to agree to work things out with one another. If your partner were unwilling to do this with you, I would recommend doing this work yourself with some help from a wise friend, therapist, or other trusted individual. I think it may seem much easier in the short run to just hit the trail and say that didn't work or this person was a jerk or worse. I would strongly recommend taking the time to explore more deeply what happened, your part, what you learned from this, and if possible, to leave with a sense of peace, healing and, strangely enough, gratitude between you and your former romantic partner. I would recommend this healing process at the end of any committed relationship. I not only recommend, but also beg you if you have kids together and are separating, agree to work through your issues for all your sakes and for what will be best for your kids. Lastly, and I know I say this often, you will probably need help with this healing and reconciliation process.

Knowing that some of the people reading this book may be at some point single or broken hearted, I have included two articles to share my journey with a broken heart and my experience with being single. If they do not pertain to you, feel free to skip to Chapter 12.

The Gift of a Broken Heart
by Hugo Elfinstone 2001

"Thank you for Loving me…thank you for breaking my heart." —Sinead O'Connor, Songwriter

I can assure you that I wouldn't have been writing about this a year ago. In all honesty I'm not sure I would have been writing about this a few weeks ago. So, if you have recently had your heart broken and are reading the words *"the gift of a broken heart"* and thinking how this seems like anything but a gift, I absolutely understand. In fact if someone had mentioned gift and broken heart in the same phrase a year ago I would have wished for them off the planet.

There are many ways to have your heart broken: the death of a friend, parent or family member, the death of a dream, or the always popular end of a relationship. The "how" doesn't matter so much…the point is, here you are and nothing can prepare you for the flood of grief, pain, anger, anxiety, depression and self-doubt that is sure to follow in waves. In fact, every broken heart is uniquely its own, so you can't even rely on the experience of past broken hearts to guide you through this time of darkness. Except that, as you may know, if you keep living, sooner or later—usually much later—this too shall pass. Which is really little consolation when you are suffering in the present and painfully clear that this is it…this is all there ever is, right here, right now…

And in truth, if you can have the courage not to fall into the self-destructive behavior of drinking, drugs, meaningless sex, over-working, or any other behavior that is a temporary escape from the pain, you are now beginning to receive the gift of living in the moment. Although it may not seem like you have received anything but immeasurable pain.

Looking back on my life I can see that I had been living with some major cracks in my heart for a long time that were old wounds that had not properly healed. I was getting by okay…and managing to have some fun moments in between mild suffering.

So, when I had my heart broken this last time, it felt like someone had set a bomb off inside me. No question my heart was properly broken. I made the choice this time to move into a cabin in the woods, continue to work, exercise, mediate, and take good care of myself even though I didn't feel like it—I wanted to die. I also refrained from all the self-destructive relief that I had used in the past.

What I found was that I was forced to just take it one day at a time, and some days I just took it moment by moment and did my best to get through the day. The pain came in waves, and that bomb that had exploded inside me brought all the times in my life that I had felt abandoned, betrayed, alone, scared and that nobody loved me to the surface.

Each time I stopped resisting the pain and allowed myself to feel feelings that I hadn't felt, I felt this intensity in my body and tears streaming from my eyes and then memories flashing in my mind. After a while it would pass and I would feel a deep sense of peace wash over me. I would look out into the world like a child for the first time, seeing this beautiful world we live in. Then I felt this wave of joy come over me and a gratitude for the gift of this life. I felt love for this whole world and all the people in it. This would last for a few days or sometimes even weeks and I would think, "I'm completely transformed and life is wonderful!"

Then shortly after would come another wave of pain and I would repeat this experience all over again. After a while I started praying, "Just let me die, I can't take this anymore. Every time I think I'm happy another wave of pain comes and washes it away."

Now I see it differently…I'm glad my heart was so completely broken because with every wave of pain that comes and I move through, I can feel a deeper sense of peace within in me. I also feel like layers and layers of superficiality about who I thought I was had been washed away. Even at some of my most painful moments I know this life is a gift and more beautiful than you could ever imagine. You just need to open your eyes and see again..

I'm not sure if I have seen the last wave or not, but I do know that I have turned the corner because I know that getting my heart properly broken has been a gift and a real healing for me.

"Thank you for Loving me…thank you for breaking my heart.."

Being Single...
by Hugo Elfinstone 2003

"Is it any less fate or destiny to be single than to be in a relationship?"

I had wanted to write this article for about six months and struggled to find the words. In the five years before I wrote this, I had been sought out for my ideas and work on relationships. Ironically, I had been single for four of the five years. .

For many of us, the idea of finding our *Life Partner*, *Soul Mate* or *Significant Other* has played a big part in our psychology and fantasy life. We hope and imagine that this is when our life would truly begin! After all, our music, movies, art and society at large suggest that this is so…"I was nothing before you, you rescued me…"

Frequently you can find words like *fate*, *destiny* and *it was meant to be* when two lovers finding each other, and this may even be true. Wouldn't it also be possible that to find your self alone (single) could very well be just as much fate, destiny, and ultimately meant to be? Instead, often the single person sees aloneness as a character fault or a cruel twist of fate, "What is wrong with me? Why is this happening to me?"

Maybe nothing is wrong, except with the images of success and happiness that are planted so deeply in our minds from so early on that lead us to believe that having a partner, kids, house, and money equals happiness. If we are observant, we can clearly see that a great deal of the folks in relationship are not happy and that a large portion often feel lonely.

Maybe it is the illusion that makes being single challenging. The romantic imagery played in our mind. The translation of the loneliness or emptiness felt inside us. We think that if we found a partner, this loneliness would cease to exist. Or would it?

From my personal experience, I can see that a relationship wouldn't fill this void (well, maybe during the honeymoon phase). On my better days, I can see that loneliness is present inside me when I am not connected to a higher source or deeper aspect of myself (I am not sure I would have any understanding of this, if I hadn't been single for the last four years).

I will also confess that there are many times I have longed for a relationship, and I imagine that there will be quite a few more. And I feel the need to point out that wanting a relationship is healthy. What becomes unhealthy is the desperation that we attach to wanting a relationship. This desperation is what can send us into deep depression, self-doubt, confusion, feelings of anxiety and hopelessness, and often sends us into the arms of the wrong kind of relationship. This desperation can also rob us of our authentic self-identity which then makes us feel incredibly lonely because we are out of touch with ourselves (and, if you like, God or our deeper self).

How to enjoy or make the most out of being single
3 steps: Acceptance, Opportunity, Finding fulfillment

Acceptance
Often we have ideas of how we think or wish our life would be. There have been countless times that I have thought, "This

isn't what my life is supposed to look like!" Yet, I can't really argue with the reality (What is…IS!). Acceptance is a very powerful first step. In acceptance, we stop resisting, and this gives us a chance to be in the reality of the present moment and frees up mental space and energy that the resistance has been filling. Countless wise people have said this is where true joy lives. I would also like to mention that accepting that you don't have a relationship today is not accepting that you will never have a relationship. It is simply surrendering to the fact that you are single now. This may allow you to see and enjoy other aspects of Life! Most of our suffering is self-induced by resisting our own reality and forming negative comparisons between our life and the lives of others.

Opportunity (Up-side)

Almost everything in life has an up-side and a down-side. I think one of the more harmful games that we can play as human beings is believing that what is not here is more important than what is here. We tend to take for granted what we do have and long for what we do not have. If we are focusing too much on wanting a relationship, we may be missing all kinds of wonderful things right in front of us. For one thing, more time is available, which brings the freedom to take a class, to get to know ourselves (or develop a deeper relationship with God), to be spontaneous, or anything else in which we find delight. The downside to relationship is that we do give up a great deal of our time and often compromise on what we want to do. Sometimes when I have been single, I would dream of having a relationship. However, in the dream, I am only looking at what the relationship will add. Then when I have gotten into a relationship, I realized that I hadn't been taking into account what would I lose. (For me there is freedom to be spontaneous, to do what I want and to go where I want).

Finding fulfillment while being single
For many of us, the words fulfillment and being single don't belong in the same sentence. Yet clearly there have been people who have a fulfilling life who were not in relationship. I think we first need to take advantage of the time and freedom that being single provides. I recommend creating some sort of a spiritual daily practice (meditation or silent prayer would be excellent). This will give you time to get more in touch with what you want in your life and possibly help to create an intimate relationship between you and the divine or deeper aspect of yourself. Next, be courageous in trying things you have always wanted to do (art, music, sports, acting, traveling, hiking, workshops, etc). Don't be afraid to go and interact with the world by yourself; get out and do things! Do some sort of exercise (twenty-thirty minutes a day). Complement that with stretching or yoga (taking a yoga or tai chi class once a week would be excellent). If you have the financial means, I would also suggest regular body work (massage, energy work, rolfing). Lastly, remember to have fun and really make the most of your existing relationships (friends, family, co-workers, etc.). Working to make all of your relationships better will help you grow and, if it comes along, be better prepared for an intimate relationship.

In conclusion: I know the courage it takes to be single. I know the strength it takes to maintain a healthy sense of self. I know it can feel lonely not to have a relationship. I know it can feel like you will be single forever (and for most of us this won't be true). I know the temptation to settle for less, and I admire anyone who holds out for the right kind of relationship. I admire anyone who has the faith to embrace this journey of being single. I admire anyone who uses this time to heal and grow. I admire anyone who takes this time to discover themselves. And lastly, I respect anyone who values themselves enough to choose to be single rather then to settle for the wrong person or a bad relationship…

Chapter 12
True Healing

I will end with a reflection on growth and relationship.

True Healing takes time and is on-going (It's not an end destination); this is both true for healing individually and in relationships.

Our nature is to grow.
The facts are simple, we are born, we live for a while, then we die. What happens before birth or after death has been debated throughout our time.
While we are alive, we are compelled towards some type of growth. You can see this in every human being on earth in some capacity.
Every human being is unique --*one of a kind*. Their inner growth is also a unique process. We each have our own specially designed course to best serve our own personal development.

The inner tensions, turmoil, and conflicts represent this pull to grow.
Acknowledgment of this process is the beginning of wisdom. Acceptance of this process is beginning of contentment.

If you wish for individual happiness, you will need to continue to grow. If you wish for relationship success, you and your partner will need to continue to grow both individually and as a couple.

If you become complacent as an individual, your life will become flat. If you become complacent as a couple, the passion will die in your relationship.

True growth, healing, and change happen on the inside first.
Worldly success doesn't always correlate to inner growth or expansion. However, inner growth will transform your life and relationships.

Thank you for reading my book!

Warmly,

Hugo Elfinstone
hugo@accesswisdom.com